Fun to do

FANCY DRESSING

Cheryl Brown & Anita Ruddell

CONTENTS

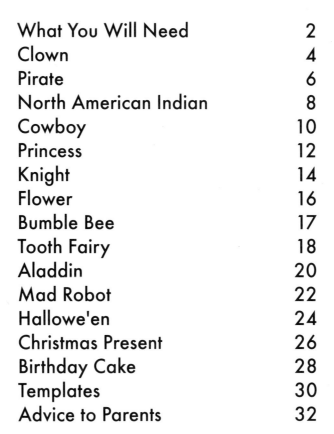

MEREHURST

What You Will Need

Whether you will be making the projects in this book for your dressing up box or to create a special costume for a fancy dress party, you should get together a few tools first. You'll need scissors or pinking shears for cutting (ask a grown up to cut thick card for you with a craft knife); a pair of compasses for making circles; a bradawl and a hole punch to make holes; glue, tape and staples to fix things together; and a needle and thread ready for sewing. Paint, felt-tip pens and fabric crayons will all come in useful for decorating.

needle and thread

clear glue

pliers

PVA glue and spreader

felt-tip pens

plastic tape

paint-brushes

clear tape

masking tape

double-sided tape

glitter glue

paint

Other Useful Things

Dressing Up Box

It is a good idea to start a collection of old clothes for dressing up in. Store them in an old basket or box. Visit jumble sales and second-hand shops. Collect all sorts of hats, scarves, bags, ties, shoes, and jewellery. Keep old pillowcases and sheets (to turn into robes) and towels and curtains (to transform into cloaks).

Face Paints

Face paints are a good way to finish off a fancy dress outfit. Some of the children in this book are wearing face paints. Have a go at trying to copy the way they look.

safety pins

tracing paper

craft knife

thick card

metal ruler

pencil and eraser

pinking shears

scissors

bradawl

stapler and staples

pair of compasses

hole punch

fabric crayons

Remember

☆ Wear an apron and cover the work area.
☆ Collect together the items in the materials box at the beginning of each project.
☆ Always ask an adult for help when you see this sign [!]
☆ Clear up after yourself.

ruler

Clown

A pair of baggy clown's trousers that come with a joke attached. Ask a friend to pull the hankie from your pocket and watch his surprise as it gets longer and longer!

Materials

pyjama trousers

wool

8 material squares

plastic-covered wire

gift ribbon

thick card 20 x 30 cm

safety pin

Hoop Trousers

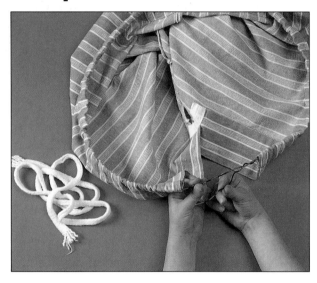

1 Replace the pyjama cord with plastic-covered wire. Twist the ends together.

2 Knot the squares of material together to make a long string. Pin to the inside of the waistband.

3 To make a 'pocket' cut a 10-cm slit on one side of the pyjamas just beneath the waistband. Pull the string of hankies through the slit.

Wig

4 Wind the wool and then the ribbon around the long edge of the card until it is covered at least twice.

5 Sew in and out of the strands of wool and ribbon along one side of the card, from one end to the other and back again.

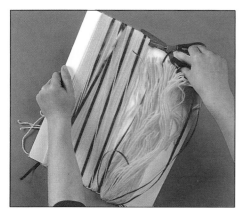

6 Cut through the wool and ribbon along the unsewn edge of the card.

Keep the wig in place with hair grips and cut a fringe at the front.

Use a small pair of braces to keep the trousers up. Choose a big, bright T-shirt to wear underneath. Gift bows make perfect 'buttons'.

Borrow Dad's shoes and use ribbons for laces.

Pirate

Before you sail the seven seas in search of treasure, take the time to make this hook and cutlass.

(see page 32)

Materials

silver foil

newspaper strips

plastic bottle

thick card

thin card

flour and water paste (see page 32)

Hook

⚠ **1** Cut the top off the plastic bottle and paint black.

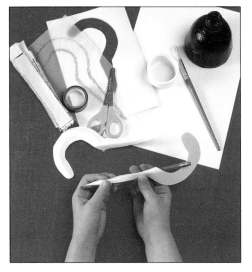

2 Trace the template on page 30 on to a folded piece of thin card. Cut out. Press each card piece around a pencil to begin to make a hook shape.

3 Twist some newspaper strips together and sandwich between the 2 pieces of card. Tape in place at the top, middle and bottom.

4 Brush the hook with paste and wrap newspaper strips around it. Put on several layers pasting in between.

Tie a scarf around your head and keep in place with an elastic band. A curtain ring makes the perfect earring.

Make this eye patch from black felt or card using the template on page 30 and attach a piece of black elastic to each side.

5 Once the hook has dried completely, cover with strips of silver foil. Push the covered hook into the neck of the bottle.

Cutlass

Use a tightly-fitting leather belt to keep your cutlass to hand.

⚠ 6 Trace off the template on pages 30-31 on to thick card and cut out. Paint the handle black and cover the blade with silver foil.

Team up a stripy T-shirt and a rolled up pair of jeans to create this pirate look.

North American Indian

Materials: thin card, fringe, ribbon, chunky wool, plastic tape, 2 elastic bands, beads, feathers, pillowcase

Invite all your friends to a pow wow. They'll need to bring a pillowcase each!

Dress

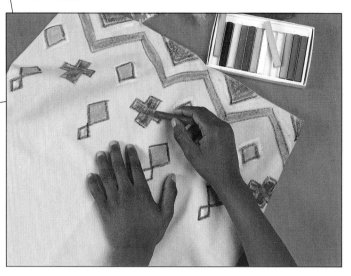

1 Make slits for your head and arms in the pillowcase. Decorate the front of the dress with fabric crayons.

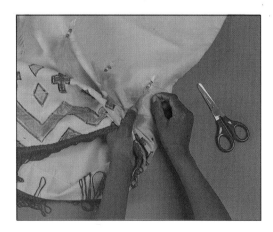

2 Sew fringe around the arm holes and along the hem of the skirt. Thread beads on to the feathers and sew on to the dress.

Headband

3 Cut a strip of card long enough to go around your head with an overlap. Decorate the front with a strip of plastic tape. Tape a feather to the back.

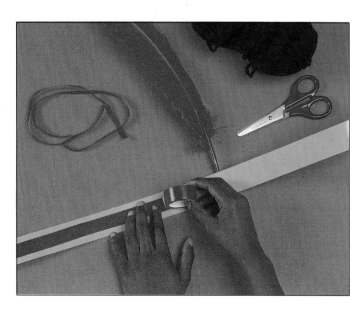

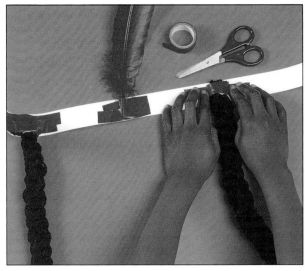

4 Cut the wool into lengths. Divide into 2 bunches. Wrap an elastic band around the top of each bunch. Plait the wool bunches. Securely tie ribbon around the bottom of each plait.

5 Tape the plaits to the inside of the headband, one on either side. Fit the finished headband around your head and staple the ends together.

To become an Indian chief, add more feathers to the headband and throw a patterned blanket across your back.

To make a papoose, follow the instructions on page 12 to make a cone from card. Decorate with fringe. Keep on your back with a long piece of cord threaded through the cone.

Cowboy

Before riding off into the sunset, you'll need a pair of spurs for your boots and a horse, of course!

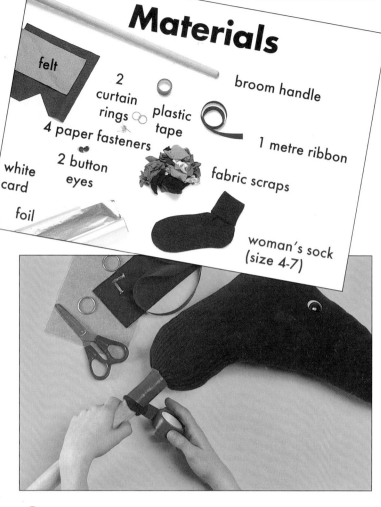

Materials

felt, 2 curtain rings, plastic tape, broom handle, 4 paper fasteners, 1 metre ribbon, white card, 2 button eyes, fabric scraps, foil, woman's sock (size 4-7)

Horse

1 Push the eyes through the toe of the sock and secure on the inside with the studs. Stuff the sock with fabric scraps.

2 Push the broom handle into the sock and wind the tape securely around it.

3 Cut a fringe along one side of a strip of felt and glue to the top of the horse's head. Cut out 2 large triangular felt ears, fold in half and sew on.

4 Thread the rings on to ribbon long enough to go around the horse's nose with a 2 cm overlap. Glue the ribbon ends together and leave to dry. Thread the remaining ribbon on to the rings and fix with paper fasteners.

Spurs

5 Cut 2 stars (template page 31) and 4 strips measuring 10 x 2 cm from the card. Cover with foil.

To complete the look, wear a cowboy hat, checked shirt, scarf and jeans; make a sheriff's badge using the template on page 31.

! **6** Sandwich each star between 2 pieces of card and use a bradawl to make a hole through the 3 layers. Push a paper fastener through the hole and open out.

To fix the spurs to your boots, stick a piece of double-sided tape to the inside of the pieces of card. Remove the backing and press firmly on to the back of each boot.

11

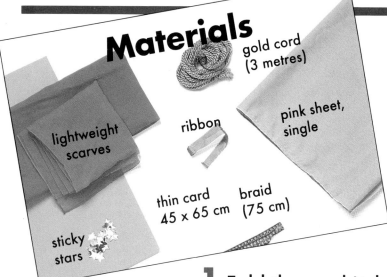

gold cord
(3 metres)

lightweight
scarves

ribbon

pink sheet,
single

thin card
45 x 65 cm

braid
(75 cm)

sticky
stars

Princess

A fairytale princess costume that can be adapted easily into a wise wizard outfit.

Cone hat

1 Fold the card in half along its longest edge. Mark on a triangle and cut out. You now have 2 card triangles the same size.

2 Lay one triangle on top of the other, so that 1.5 cm of the bottom triangle can be seen. Put double-sided tape along this edge, take off the backing and fold over on to the top triangle. Press firmly down. Turn over and repeat.

3 Trim the brim into a circle by cutting off the pointed ends. Decorate the cone with sticky stars all over and glue braid around the brim.

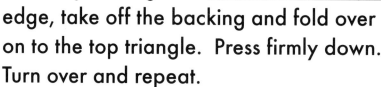

4 Snip off the top of the cone. Push the scarves into the hole and tape to the inside.

Robe

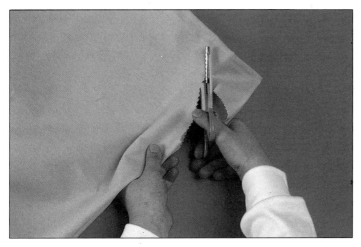

⚠ **5** Fold the sheet in half widthways, then in half again lengthways. To make an opening for your head, make a small triangular cut across the folded corner of the sheet with pinking shears.

Tape ribbon to the inside to tie on the hat.

Make a cloak from an old curtain. Thread with cord. Wrap around your shoulders and tie the cord under your chin.

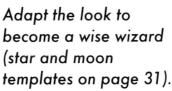

Adapt the look to become a wise wizard (star and moon templates on page 31).

⚠ **6** Slip the sheet over your head. Wrap the cord around your waist, cross over your chest, and take over your shoulders. Cross the cord over your back and bring around to the front of your waist. Tie in a knot.

Knight

A few *trusty snips of the scissors and some bold bits of gluing will turn you into a brave knight.*

pillowcase

red felt

1 cm wide elastic

silver foil

5 paper fasteners

silver card

2 silver-sprayed dishcloths

thick card

Tunic

1 Make slits in the pillowcase for your arms and head. Cut 4 strips from the red felt. Snip a triangle into the end of each strip and stick on to the front of the tunic to make a cross.

Shield

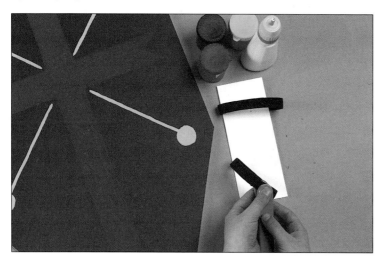

2 Draw a shield on to the card and cut out. Paint the front of the shield and leave to dry. Cut 2 pieces of elastic to fit around your forearm and staple into hoops.

3 Thread the hoops on to the card strip and glue on to the back of the shield.

Helmet

4 Staple a silver dishcloth to the centre of a silver card band, measuring 60 x 5 cm. Fit the band around your head and staple the ends together.

5 Fix a 30 x 4 cm strip of silver card from one side of the headband to the other using paper fasteners. Now fix a strip measuring 50 x 4 cm from the back to the front of the headband, leaving a bit of card hanging down at the front.

Slip the tunic over an outfit of grey sweatshirt, jogging bottoms, and wellington boots covered with silver foil. Wear a pair of grey woollen gloves.

6 Put the helmet on and ask a friend to mark the shape of your nose on to the nose bar. Cut out. Shape some foil into a dome to fit the inside of the helmet and tape in place. Staple the second dishcloth in place.

To finish off the shield spray a large plastic pot lid with silver paint and glue to the centre.

Cut a 15-cm slit at the centre of the bottom edge of the front of the tunic.

15

Flower

Two perfect party costumes for you and a friend. But who will bloom and who will buzz?

Materials

green card strip

red paper

green bin liner

paper plate

thin white elastic

crêpe paper

1 Cut out the centre of the paper plate. Paint yellow and leave to dry. Glue small pink crêpe paper petals to the back of the plate rim, and large red paper petals on top of the crêpe petals. Attach thin elastic to each side to keep in place.

Slip the dress over your head and secure at the back of the neck with a safety pin.

Use double-sided tape to keep the belt in place around your waist.

2 Use pinking shears to cut out large leaves from the green crêpe paper. Make slits in the bin liner for your head and arms. Staple a leaf to each shoulder.

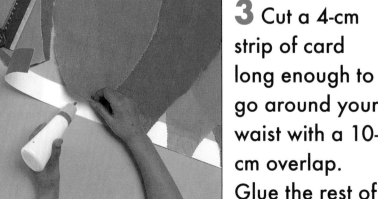

3 Cut a 4-cm strip of card long enough to go around your waist with a 10-cm overlap. Glue the rest of the leaves to the back of the card strip.

16

Bumble Bee

Materials

black elastic

gold glitter pen

black tights

plastic-covered wire

black plastic tape

cotton wool

1 Bend 1 metre of wire into a hoop. Make another wire hoop. Join the hoops by twisting the ends together. Cover the twisted ends with cotton wool padding and keep in place with tape.

Thread a long pipe cleaner through the weave on top of a black balaclava. Sew a yellow bobble to each end.

Wear the bumble bee wings over an outfit of black leggings and a black sweatshirt that has had yellow ribbon strips double-sided across the front of it.

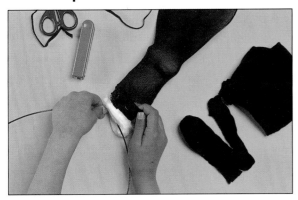

2 Cut the legs from the tights and stretch over the wire hoops. Overlap and tape together. Cut 2 40-cm pieces of black elastic and staple into hoops. Slip over the wings and tape to either side of the padded bar.

3 Reshape the wire hoops. Decorate by gluing lines of glitter over the front of the wings.

17

Tooth Fairy

Turn an old net curtain into a wonderful pair of glittering fairy wings.

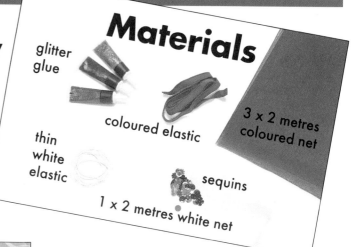

Materials

glitter glue

coloured elastic

thin white elastic

3 x 2 metres coloured net

sequins

1 x 2 metres white net

Wings

1 Use glitter glue to decorate the white net with swirling patterns. Hang up to dry.

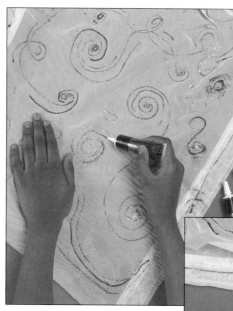

2 Sew 2 lines of running stitches up the centre of the net, leaving long threads at either end. Gently pull the threads to gather the net and secure with a knot.

3 Make 2 loops from white elastic large enough to go around your wrists and sew to the top 2 corners of the wings.

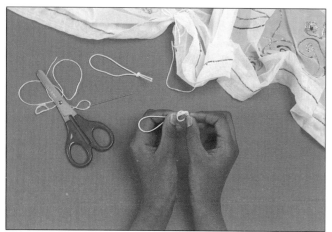

Skirt

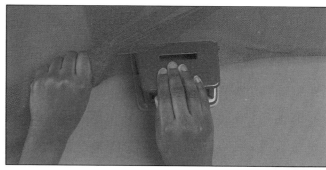

4 Fold the coloured net in half. Punch holes along the folded edge.

5 Carefully thread the coloured elastic through the punched holes. Knot the ends of the elastic together to fit around your waist.

To transform yourself into a butterfly, make a pair of wings from a piece of old white sheet decorated with fabric paints. Twist 2 pipe cleaners around a hairband and curl the ends.

To make a tooth necklace thread polystyrene packing chips on to coloured cotton. Don't forget to take a bag to carry your tooth money in!

Make a wand from a garden stick stuck into a star cut out from corrugated cardboard (template page 31). Cover with silver foil.

6 Glue sequins all over the skirt and hang up to dry.

Wear your fairy wings and skirt over a brightly-coloured pair of tights and matching top. Use safety pins to pin the wings to the back of the top and slip the elastic hoops over your wrists.

19

Aladdin

If you've always wanted to be an Arabian prince or princess, you don't need a genie to make your wish come true. Just follow these simple instructions...

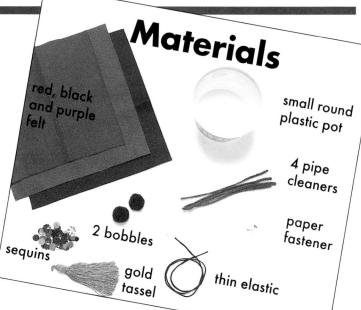

Materials

red, black and purple felt

small round plastic pot

4 pipe cleaners

paper fastener

sequins

2 bobbles

gold tassel

thin elastic

Fez

1 Draw around the base of the pot on to red felt and cut out. Fix the tassel to the felt circle with a paper fastener.

2 Cut a strip of red felt wide and long enough to go around the pot with a small overlap and glue in place. Trim the felt at the base to make it even.

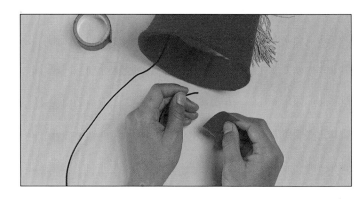

3 Cut slits along the felt at the top and base of the pot. Put glue on the felt tabs. Stick the glued tabs to the inside and base of the pot.

4 Glue the felt circle to the base of the pot. Tape a piece of elastic to either side of the pot on the inside.

20

Slippers

5 Cut 2 triangles from black felt and 2 from purple felt (template on page 30).

6 Glue 2 pipe cleaners along the long edges of a purple triangle. Glue a black triangle on top. Repeat with the other 2 triangles.

For Aladdin's trousers, take an old pair of silky adult pyjama bottoms and sew some elastic into the hem.

7 To decorate the slippers glue sequins on top of the black triangles. Sew a bobble to the tip. Bend the end of the slippers into a curl. Attach to a pair of plimsoles with double-sided tape.

To become an Arabian princess drape yourself in silky material.

Wrap a silk scarf around your waist and keep in place with a brooch.

21

Mad Robot

Recycle your rubbish and turn yourself into a mad robot.

Body

⚠ **1** Cut the flaps from the box. Cut holes in the top and side of the box large enough for your head and arms to go through. Glue the packaging to the box.

Keep any gold or coloured foil packaging aside for later.

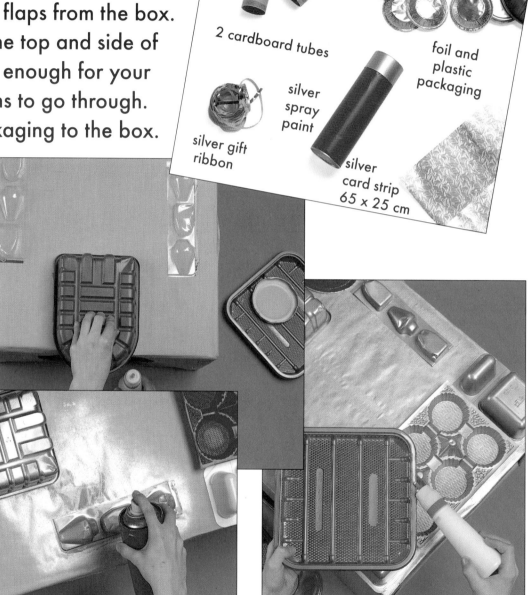

Materials

large cardboard box

2 cardboard tubes

silver gift ribbon

silver spray paint

foil and plastic packaging

silver card strip 65 x 25 cm

⚠ **2** Spray the box and the 2 cardboard tubes with the silver spray paint.

3 Glue the gold and coloured foil packaging to the box.

22

4 Cut a letterbox slit in the centre of the card strip for you to see out of. Overlap the ends of the card strip to make a tube and staple together.

5 Cut a round hole on either side large enough to push the silver cardboard tubes into. Curl the silver ribbon using closed scissor blades and tape to the inside of the tube.

Wear the body over an outfit of grey jogging bottoms and grey sweatshirt. Cover a pair of wellington boots with silver foil.

Cut the top and bottom off of 2 plastic bottles. Spray with silver paint. Wear over a pair of plastic household gloves that have also been sprayed silver. Alternatively wear a pair of grey woollen gloves.

23

Hallowe'en

Three super scary looks that are so good you won't want to wait until Hallowe'en to try them out!

Witch's hat

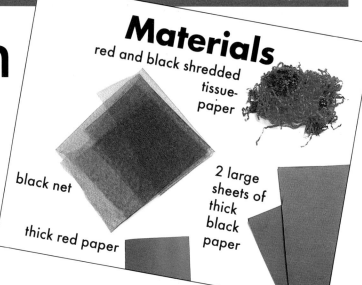

Materials

red and black shredded tissue-paper

black net

thick red paper

2 large sheets of thick black paper

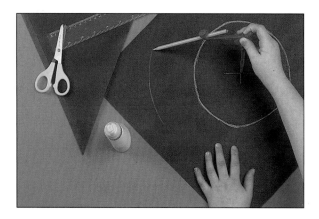

1 Make a cone from 1 sheet of paper (see page 12). Draw around the base of the cone on to the second sheet of paper. Draw on another circle 7 cm larger in diameter than the first.

2 Use a ruler to divide the inner circle into 8 equal sections. Starting from the centre, cut along these lines and bend back the triangular tabs.

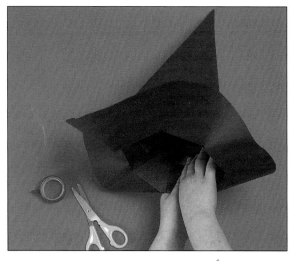

3 Put the cone over the brim. Tape the tabs to the inside.

4 Glue shredded paper all around the brim of the hat, leaving a

small opening for your face.

24

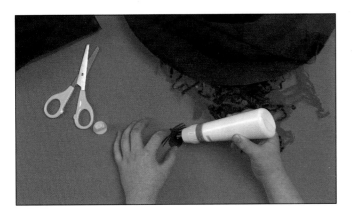

5 Tape a triangle of net from the top of the cone to the brim to make a spider's web. Glue red and black paper spiders (templates page 30) to the net.

Ghost

Cut 2 eye holes in an old sheet. For a really spooky effect, paint a ghoulish face on to the sheet with fabric paints.

Witch

Cut openings for your head and arms in a black bin liner. Cut star and moon shapes from gold and silver paper (templates page 31) and glue to the front of the bin liner.

Dracula

Wear a black sweatshirt over a white shirt and a pair of black jogging bottoms. For the cloak, cut a zig-zag pattern along one edge of a bin liner and pin it to the arms and back of the sweatshirt. Make a bow tie from a piece of white crêpe paper held at the centre with a hoop of white card stapled in place.

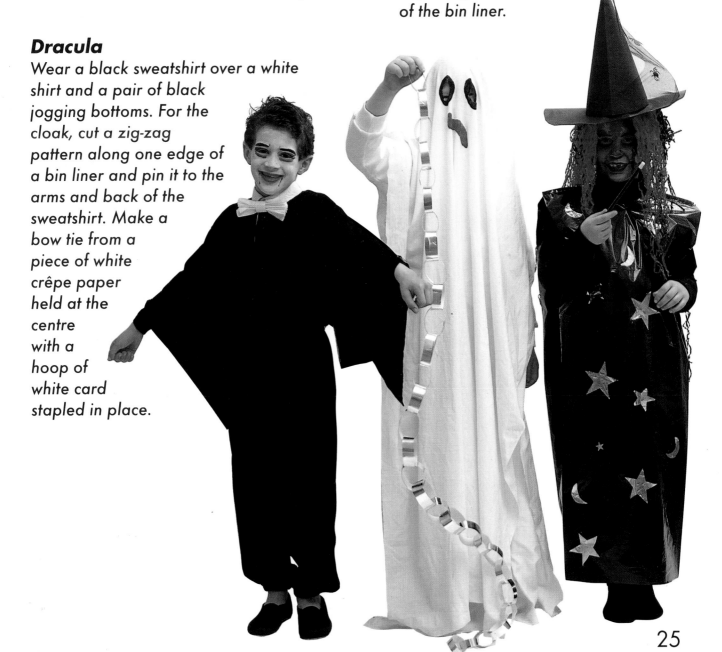

Christmas Present

Give your friends and family a surprise by wrapping yourself up for Christmas.

Materials

printed wrapping paper

large cardboard box

metallic paper

gift ribbon

Christmas card

⚠ 1 Cut the flaps from the box. Cut holes for your arms and head. Cover with wrapping paper.

2 At the head and arm openings cut triangular tabs from the paper. Glue the tabs to the inside of the box.

3 For a decorative ribbon glue wide strips of metallic paper around the box.

4 Cut a large square of metallic paper. Fold over the edge of the paper by 2 cm and press down. Turn over and fold over by 2 cm again. Repeat until all the paper has been folded.

6 Punch a hole in the top left-hand corner of the Christmas card. Thread the ribbon through the hole.

5 Fold in half and staple the top 2 edges together to make a fan. Put a length of double-sided tape along the bottom of the fan, remove the backing and press down firmly on to the box to the side of the head hole.

Tie the Christmas card gift tag around your wrist.

Wear the Christmas present over an outfit of leotard and tights or sweatshirt and jogging bottoms.

To make a decoration for your hair, stick a rosette to a hair slide. Curl lengths of thin metallic ribbon along closed scissor blades and tie to the slide.

Birthday Cake

Next time you are invited to a fancy dress birthday party, why not go as the cake!

Materials

large sheet thin white card

wrapping paper

crêpe frill

2 1-metre lengths of ribbon

cake frill

cake candles

cake candle holders

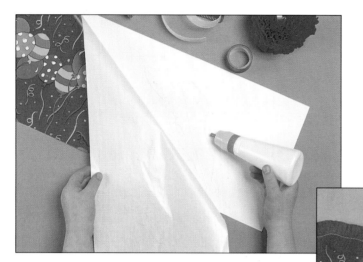

Body frill

1 Cut 2 strips of card measuring 20 cm wide. Cover with wrapping paper. Tape the decorated card strips together to make one long strip.

2 Glue crêpe frill along the top and bottom edge of the strip.

3 Staple the ends of the decorated strip together to make a hoop. To make braces, staple the ribbons to the hoop crossing them over at the back.

Hat

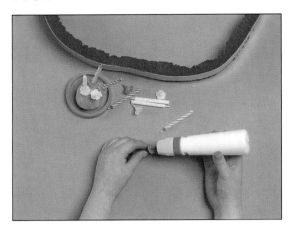

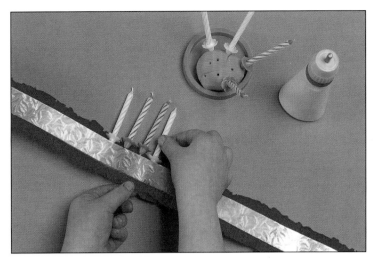

4 Glue the candles into the holders. Leave to dry.

5 Push the holders into the cake frill along the top edge and glue in place.

Cut a number from felt to match the age of the birthday boy or girl. Put double-sided tape along the back of the felt number. Remove the backing from the double-sided tape and press the felt number firmly on to your chest.

6 Fit the cake frill around your head and staple the ends together.

Wear the birthday cake over an outfit of brightly coloured leotard or T-shirt and leggings.

! IMPORTANT: The candles on the cake frill hat are just for show. Do not light them.

Templates

For instructions on how to trace a
template turn to page 32.

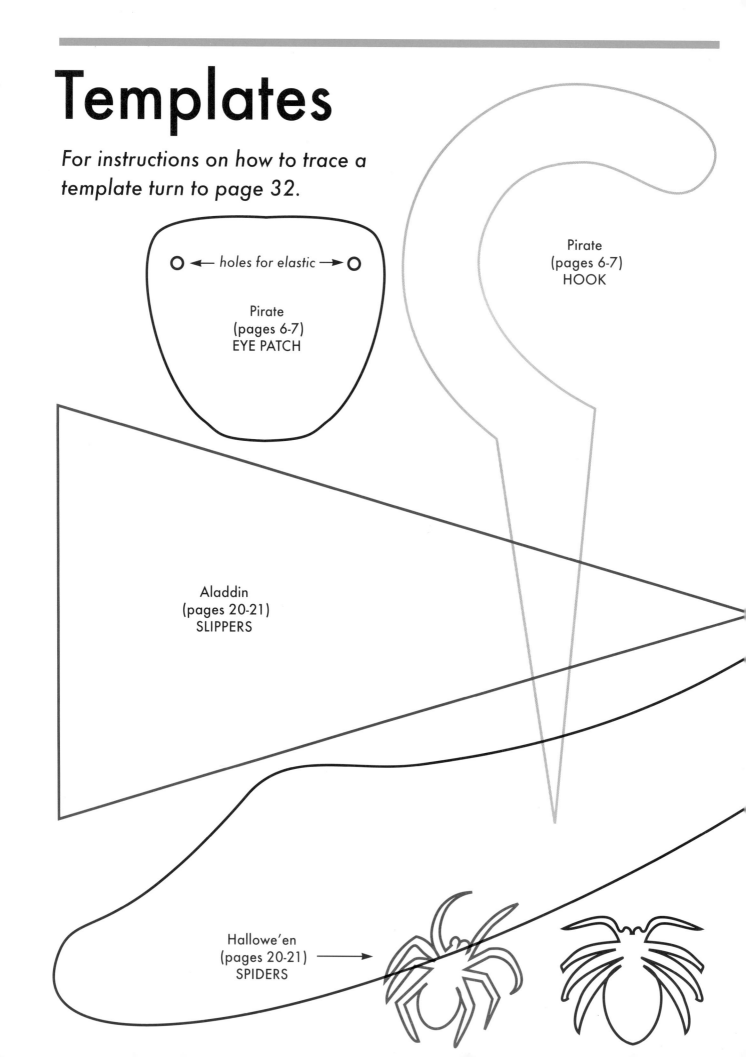

O ← *holes for elastic* → O

Pirate
(pages 6-7)
EYE PATCH

Pirate
(pages 6-7)
HOOK

Aladdin
(pages 20-21)
SLIPPERS

Hallowe'en
(pages 20-21)
SPIDERS

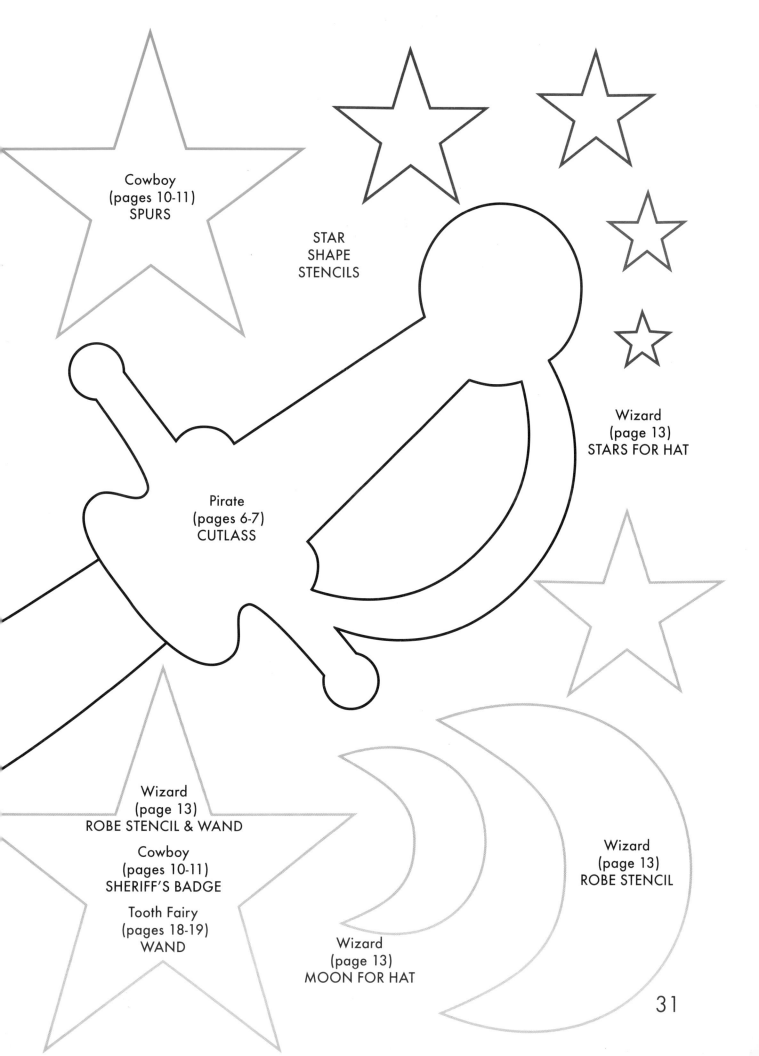

Cowboy
(pages 10-11)
SPURS

STAR
SHAPE
STENCILS

Wizard
(page 13)
STARS FOR HAT

Pirate
(pages 6-7)
CUTLASS

Wizard
(page 13)
ROBE STENCIL & WAND

Cowboy
(pages 10-11)
SHERIFF'S BADGE

Tooth Fairy
(pages 18-19)
WAND

Wizard
(page 13)
MOON FOR HAT

Wizard
(page 13)
ROBE STENCIL

31

Advice to Parents

Many of the fancy dress outfits in this book are based on items of clothing that can be found in any child's wardrobe, or sometimes the wardrobe of his or her parent! Sweatshirts, jogging bottoms, leotards and swimming costumes, tights or leggings, T-shirts, balaclavas and gloves, a pair of braces, plimsoles and wellington boots all have a part to play. But none of these things is essential, so don't rush out to the shops with your chequebook. After all the magical thing about dressing up is that children can transform themselves into a king or a queen, a hero or a heroine, with their imagination alone. The project ideas in this book aim to help them bring their imaginings to life. Most of the projects in this book can be made with things that can be found around the home: food packaging, plastic bottles, old sheets and pillowcases, odd socks, bin liners, dishcloths, to name just a few. The information on this page is designed to help you to encourage your child to get the most from these projects.

Tools and Materials

Paint From a small selection of paints – red, yellow, blue, black and white – all other colours can be obtained by mixing. Encourage your child to explore colour mixing for herself. Add a drop of washing-up liquid to the paint when painting over plastic. Always help your child when using spray paints. Put small items in a cardboard box and spray. Larger items should be sprayed outdoors if possible.

Glue Solvent-free PVA adhesive is recommended.

Tape A wide range of tapes will come in useful, in particular double-sided tape and plastic tape. Double-sided tape comes in rolls in various widths and can be bought from a stationers or art and craft shop. It offers a perfect alternative to glue on fabric when a temporary join is all that is required. It is rather expensive but worth every penny. If you use it carefully it will go a long way. Plastic tape (or insulating tape as it is also called) comes in a wide range of bright colours. Not only can it be used to join things together, but it can also be used very effectively for decoration. It is available from DIY and hardware stores.

Scissors For the sake of safety children should use small scissors with round-ended metal blades and plastic handles. Although these are fine for cutting paper and thin card, they will not cut thick card and this is best done by you. This will often require a craft knife. Use a metal ruler to provide a straight cutting edge. If you do not have a cutting mat, use an old chopping board or very thick card to protect the work surface beneath. Regularly change the craft knife blade for a clean, sharp edge.

Bradawl An ideal tool for making a hole in card. Lay the card over a flattened ball of play dough or modelling clay and pierce with the bradawl.

Fabric crayons and paints These are an ideal way to transform old sheets and pillowcases into fancy dress clothes. There are many makes available, and we have found that the fabric crayons are easiest to use for this age group. Once a drawn design has been fixed by ironing, the decorated items are washable. For more detailed advice on the use of these products you are advised to refer to the manufacturer's instructions.

Glitter glue A quick and easy way to add decoration to both fabric and paper, glitter glue is available in pen or tube form in a wide range of colours from red and green to gold and orange. Any large newsagents or stationers should stock a selection.

Papier mâché is made from old newspapers and a flour and water paste. To make this smooth, slightly runny paste you will need approximately 2 heaped tablespoons of plain white flour to 100 ml water. Gradually add the water to the flour and mix well.

Pair of compasses is a good tool for marking out a perfect circle. The diameter of a circle is the measurement taken across its centre. The pair of compasses needs to be fixed at half the measurement of the diameter. Keep the point firmly in contact with the paper and slowly move the pencil arm around to form the circle. Alternatively draw around a dinner plate to make a large circle, or a tea plate to make an average sized circle, or a yoghurt pot for a small circle.

A Word About Face Paints

Water-based face paints are available as crayons or paints. The paints, which come in individual pots or palettes, will give more detailed results. The base paint should be evenly applied with a piece of sponge and finer detail added with a brush. Before applying face paints, you should always check that the child's skin is not allergic to them. Water-based face paints can be removed easily with soap and water.

Making a Tracing

To make a tracing from the templates on pages 30-31 lay a piece of tracing paper over the required template. Draw around the outline with a pencil. Turn over the tracing paper and scribble over the pencil outline. Turn the tracing paper over once again and lay it down on to the paper or card that you want to transfer the tracing to. Carefully draw around the pencil outline. Remove the tracing paper. The outline of the traced shape on the card may be quite faint. Go over it with black felt-tip pen if necessary. To make a reusable template transfer the tracing on to thick card. Cut out and label the card template and keep it in a safe place. Use the card template to draw around as often as it is needed.

Published 1994 by Merehurst Limited
Ferry House, 51-57 Lacy Road, Putney, London SW15 1PR

© Copyright 1994 Merehurst Limited
ISBN 1 898018 25 1

Project Editor: Cheryl Brown
Designer: Anita Ruddell
Photography by Jon Bouchier
Face painting by Juliet Appleyard
Colour separation by P & W Graphics Pty Ltd, Singapore
Printed in Italy by G.Canale & C. SpA

The publisher would like to thank the staff and children of Riversdale Primary School, London Borough of Wandsworth, for their help in producing the photographs for this book.